THE WORLD ACCORDING TO DAD FOR NEWLYWEDS

The World According To Dad For Newlyweds
A Lindos Books/January 2003

Published in the United States by Lindos Books.

Book Design by Sandra A. Autorino, Live Oak Productions

Library of Congress Cataloging-in-Publication Data

Mantis, Constantine M., 1951 -
The World According To Dad: A Manual for the Good Life
1. Mantis, Constantine M., 1951 - 2. Personal Growth, Self-improvement aspects. 3. Values; Ethical and Spiritual aspects.
I. Title

ISBN 0-9672875-2-9
2002094018
CIP

1 2 3 4 5 6 7 8 9 10
Revised Edition

Printed in the United States

THE WORLD ACCORDING TO DAD FOR NEWLYWEDS

Revised Edition, Originally Published as
THE WORLD ACCORDING TO DAD

C.M. MANTIS

C.M. Mantis was born Constantine Michael Mantis on a farm in Pennsylvania in 1951. He began work at the age of 6 in the family restaurant. His love of the land and respect for the diversity of mankind forged lasting, lifelong impressions on his heart and mind. Simple pleasures and major accomplishments have filled his life.

He owned his first business in 1966, a boardwalk burger stand on the Jersey shore. Profits bought land. He graduated from Phillips Exeter in 1969; was married in San Francisco in 1970. He shared the birth of his daughter, painted and showed his first one-man exhibit, graduated from Albright College with a BFA and completed his first feature film, all in 1974. "Reading 1974: Portrait of a City" was called "1 of the 10 best films of 1975" by Film Comment Magazine. It aired on PBS and at the Museum of Modern Art and is housed in the permanent collection of MOMA and The Reading Public Museum.

He received his MFA in Film from Yale University in 1977 and has worked successfully in the entertainment business the past 25 years. His first feature film in Hollywood was for Roger Corman, John Davidson and Joe Dante, as Background Director on "Piranha". He has written numerous screenplays, most notably "Time of Tears", a low budget feature film he also directed in 1983. It was picked up and distributed by New World Pictures.

He shared the Emmy for "The Murder of Mary Phagan" as Best Miniseries for 1987-88. Varied jobs have included feature films, documentaries, off-off Broadway, commercials, industrials and educationals.

His entrepreneurial efforts include Alpha Chips in New York City in 1983, the chocolate chip cookie company from space. His original character, Alphaman, and his shiny white rocketship bikes captured local and international press (NBC, CBS, ABC, NY Times, Wall Street Journal, National Public Radio, International Herald-Tribune, etc.) for design, chutzpah and heart. Alphaman was the cover story and photo of Nikkei Business Magazine, "1 of 10 best new businesses in America in 1984." In June of 1985, he opened his first Alphaman franchise in Tokyo, Japan. In 1992, CM took a business plan for a pizza delivery operation, Pizza Pie in the Sky Pizza, to Myrtle Beach and disappeared into the tall grasses of the South Carolina low country. In 1998, he opened a real-estate appraisal company in Stamford, Connecticut with a cousin.

His greatest accomplishment, however, has been as a father. No challenge has been greater than being a divorced dad. No award has exceeded the simple joys of fatherhood. The World According to Dad, a Manual for the Good Life is the culmination of 25 years of extensive, first hand 'dad' research. Simple yet extraordinary, Dad opens the dialogue on values, love, family and God, certain to continue for years to come.

For more information, interviews and speaking engagements, please contact Lindos Books at 877.773.8884 or visit the website at www.worlddad.com

Also by the author:

The World According To Dad, A Manual for the Good Life

The World According To Dad For Teenagers, A Manual for the Good Life

The World According To Dd For Newlyweds, A Manual for the Good Life

The World According To Dad For Parents, A Manual for the Good Life

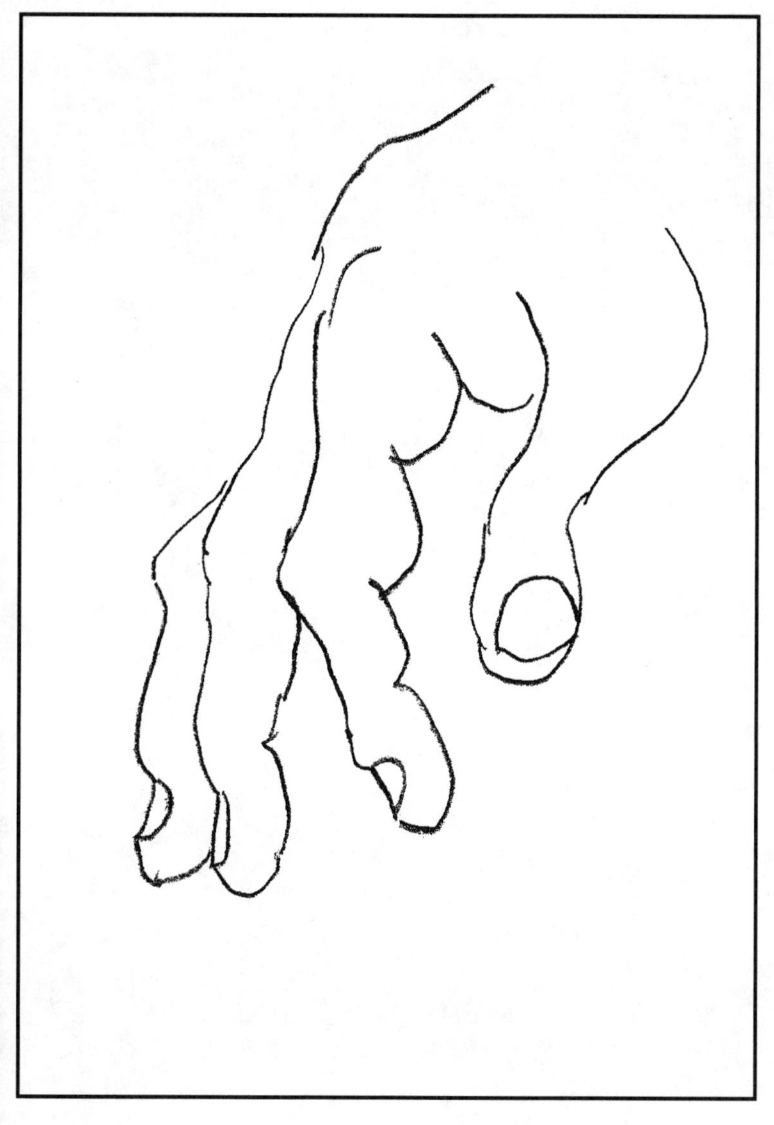

DEDICATION

To Meg and Bob,

May this little book inspire you

to live the precious gift of life with all you've got.

I love you.

Dad

ACKNOWLEDGMENTS

Forty-eight years of living have honed and shaped me through trail and error, victory and defeat, agony and joy. I am forever indebted to the strong and loving hands and hearts of those women and men I call my mentors. Many more have touched my life than can be acknowledged. For those unnamed, you know who you are and that I love you.

For Coach Daub, my junior high school football coach, who taught me the power of mind over matter. He made me believe we could be the city champs.

For Harry Koursaros, my painting teacher, who taught me to be bold in my art and create from the heart.

For Rich DeVos, the world's greatest "cheerleader", who taught me the power of giving and uplifting others.

For Mom, who raised a beautiful, loving family and taught me tenacity, persistence and the pursuit of excellence.

For Dad, who lived by faith and belief and an indomitable positive spirit and taught me to follow my dreams and never give up.

For Meg, without her, I wouldn't be a Dad.

And for God, without Him, I wouldn't be.

SPECIAL THANKS

I am indebted to the help of so many along the way these first few years of writing, publishing and speaking. Friends and family have given me food and lodging for days at a time as I tour the country. Others have turned out for signings and events and bought books and told their friends. Many have cheered me on. Words don't do justice to the gratitude I feel. Thank you, dear friends. And there are those whose contributions have been herculean.

I thank Stephen Engratt for his belief and time and impeccable attention to detail as my editor. He has made my work better.

I thank Sandy Autorino for her endless hours designing, creating and formatting to make such a beautiful book for my daughter and son, and now for all to enjoy.

I thank my dear friend, Mike Edwards, who has believed in me from the very beginning. His generosity, friendship and inspiration have been instrumental to my success.

I thank my little Yaya, who has always been there for me with comfort and love and tomatoes and feta, those basic necessities of life.

I thank my dear Aunt Christine who has worked so tirelessly for me, always with a joke and smile.

And I thank Bubbie for her undying love, belief and support. Thanks for being such a great Mom.

I am the luckiest man in the world to have such family and friends. Thank you. I couldn't do this without you.

CONTENTS

Revised Edition, Originally Published as, THE WORLD ACCORDING TO DAD

INTRODUCTION

There are certain times and certain events in our lives that we call milestones, the first step, the first word, the first tooth, the first day at school, the first job. For Moms and Dads everywhere, our lives are marked by such moments. In 1998, I experienced one of those moments that changed my life forever – and the lives of many others, as fate would have it. My one and only daughter got married.

On the surface, it may not seem like a big deal. People get married every day. True. But for a Dad, a single, divorced Dad who loves his daughter and was there for her all the way, it was a really big deal.

It all started the year before, in 1997. Meg, my daughter, had graduated the University of Georgia in '96 and gone to work for Ernest and Young in Atlanta. I was so proud of her, and still am, of course. In '97, she called to tell me that she had met a really great guy, also at the firm, and it was getting pretty serious and they would like to come see me in New York where I was living and working at the time.

Well, "the kids" came to New York. Meg and Bob came all the way from Atlanta, Georgia to New York City to meet me in person and get my approval for their wedding plans. I was so impressed and so moved that they had so much respect and love that they would make such a long journey. Heck, today we email or leave a message or send a note if we have something important to say because we're so darn busy, but to travel 900 miles to see me in person – wow!

Technically speaking, I guess my moment, my milestone, began that night in New York City, but I'm not sure I totally realized the life-changing importance of that moment until much later. There we were in the New York City night, hugging, kissing, laughing and crying tears of joy right on Fifth Avenue in the Big Apple. We just had to celebrate so we jumped in the car and took off for the Windows on the World at the World Trade Center, making photo stops at Rockefeller Center and Times Square along the way. I always carried a camera with me as Meg was growing up so I could "capture the moment." I had one that night, too.

Champagne bubbles and raised glasses mingled with more smiles and tears of joy. We called my Mom – Meg's grandmom, "Bubbie" to share the news. Meg is her first grandchild and very special to her and my Dad died back in '95, so it was a really special moment for Bubbie, too.

Driving home that night, I steered my way through smiling tears and thanked God for all the incredible blessings He had given me, especially for this daughter – and son(to-be) – who had so much respect and love for this Dad that they took the time out of their busy modern lives to come and see me in person.

I've always been a spiritual kind of guy and believed in God, in a higher power and order in Universe, so when I got home I felt compelled to pray again. I got on my knees and humbled myself and gave thanks. My heart was so full. Something came over me and as I was thanking God for this incredible gift of love, I asked Him what He had in mind for me when He put me on this Earth. It turned out to be a life-changing question. I said, "God, you've given me a wonderful life filled with blessings, but I don't think ever once asked you what you had in mind for me. I always knew best. I always did it my way. But I'm asking you now, God, why did you put me here? So if it's not too late and you're not too pissed off, please tell me what you want me to do and I promise I will do it to the very best of my ability. I won't have a better idea. I won't try to do it my way. I will be your humble servant. I will do what you want me to do. Thank you, God. Amen."

Several weeks later, in His own way and time, He answered my prayer. He told me He wanted me to write and speak. I just said, "Sure. Absolutely. What do you want me to write?" He told me, "Tell your daughter what she needs to know." I said, "Okay," and went right home and got to work.

As I set out to tell my daughter "what she needs to know," I was forced to ask myself, "What do we need to know? What is really important in life?" So I wrote this little book about "the really important things in life" and gave it to Meg and Bob on their wedding day. What a day! What a gift! I felt like the richest man in the world. Selfishly, I felt extra special proud because I had done what God told me to do. I was a good servant. Little did I know that my mission had just begun.

Over the next year, family and friends read the book and were so inspired that they said I had to publish. I listened to that for a year and finally gave the manuscript to some strangers to read and they all asked, "When is it coming out?" That did it. I called "the kids" and asked them what they thought. They said, "Dad, we love you, we love the book. Go for it!" So I did.

Since 2000, I have appeared at over 300 bookstores and events across the U.S., sharing this book about "the really important things in life." Thousands of lives have been touched and so many more hearts have been inspired and changed. As I traveled the country and shared with others, I began to realize that this is what God had in mind for me. He said He wanted me to write and speak. Today, that is what I do.

The World According to Dad, A Manual for the Good Life has been so successful that it has naturally transformed itself into a series of "manuals for the good life." We have gotten off track with our rush to materialism and the pursuit of the "politically correct." In truth, that does not work. Money and politics were created by man to control and manipulate others, simple manifestations of the self-centered, control-freak ego. Why do so many people seem confused and unhappy and living on Prozac? I believe it is because we have allowed ourselves to be misled by the glitz and bought into materialism as a road to happiness. Well, if money makes us happy, and we in America are the richest people in the world, why isn't everybody supremely happy?

Why we are not happy is because we have neglected "the really important things in life." We are so busy making money to buy things and pay bills that we don't even have time for our children. Kids don't need money or things, kids need love and touch and that has to be given in person. It's impossible to give love when we're not home because we're too busy. Hello!!! Are you really too busy to love? Like a plant must have water and sun, humans must have love and touch. Take away love and touch – because we're too busy – and what happens to humans? I didn't want my daughter and son(in-law) going down that empty road. I love them too much.

What I gave to them, I now offer to you. Just ask yourself, can you really live a quality, good life without love? Without integrity? Without respect? Without hope?

Hopefully you, too, will realize that there is more to life than money and greed and you will take a stand for "the really important things in life." This is your life. It is your choice. I challenge you to do the right thing. And please email or write me to let me know that you know what's "really important in life."

You can do it. You are the only you in this whole wide universe. You were made for greatness. Go ahead, do the right thing. You can make a difference.

Keep up the good work,

C.M. "Dad" Mantis
17956 Canby Road
Leesburg, VA 20175
dad@worlddad.com

THE WORLD ACCORDING TO DAD FOR NEWLYWEDS

LIFE

Fall seven times,
stand up eight.

JAPANESE PROVERB

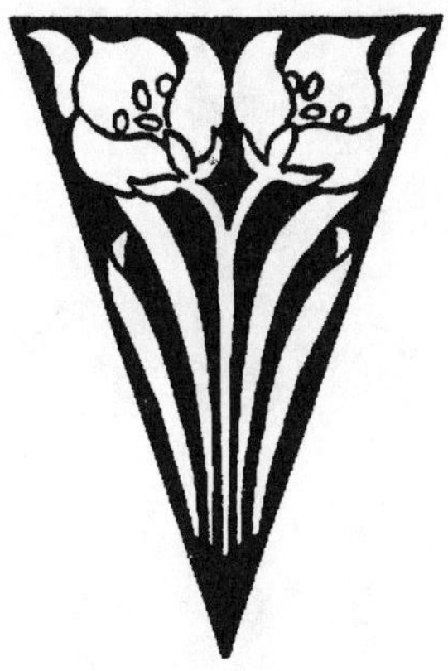

LIFE

Hey, kiddo:

What's up? How was your first day at the firm? I know you did great. You, in your crisp-pressed suit, fresh leather briefcase, unscuffed by the years to come, ready to take on life and make your mark. I'm so proud of you. I wish I could have been there. You'll have to tell me all about it.

So listen, something funny happened to me today. It wasn't so much funny, ha ha, as it was weird. It was a beautiful day; a gray, crisp, clear defining winter day, and I was on this winding country road – you know how I like the backroads, rolling hills, patchwork fields, naked black treelines, fieldrock walls, silos, barns, hex signs and colors so rich with the radio playing and just loving life. Good times rushed through my mind in pictures of the heart. And this Voice said, "be quiet". Now I'm not sure what that meant, but before I could think my hand reached out and turned the radio off. It was playing the Eagles – and I like the Eagles – but I turned it off anyway, and it was quiet. Just wheels hitting the blacktop and my mind full with life.

And there I was wheels on the road, wheel in my hand, wheel in my mindheart turning pictures of you and me, dad and kid, living, feeling, growing, kicking, fighting, laughing, loving life.

Remember that cradle I made for you when you were still in your mom's tummy with the crescent mahogany moon cut out of the sides and the sweeping wave headboard and foot? I mean you probably don't remember it first hand exactly, you were just a baby. But I know you've seen that cradle picture – baby infant you looking through that crescent moon. That picture's been hanging on my wall for the past twenty-four years.

And remember our Katahdin trip? You, knock-kneed and skinned knees, crossing the Knife's Edge and taking that mountain, you only eight years old.

Remember Saturday night pizza card shark parties in Times Square?

And that road trip down the Atlantic Coast, Cape May to Ocracoke and back up the Blue Ridge skyline?

And thc Mermaid Parade and Nathan's french fries at Coney Island? And cross-country driving to our North Branch farm in the Ontario bush? Or how about hiking the Grand Canyon and Glacier National Park, road-tripping the Canadian maritimes to P.E.I. with your cousin Samantha, riding rocketbikes on the streets of New York, ball games at Yankee Stadium, New Year's Eve in Times Square, walking the midnight ice at Mohonk, camping out in the Keys, telling stories, singing songs, having fun, living life? Remember, kiddo?

And there I am, just driving along with the radio off, loving the landscapes and mindscapes, my heart filled up, just driving and smiling at you and me, and life. All I can say is, thank you, God, for this wonderful life. I almost feel guilty I'm feeling so good, but I don't believe in guilt so I just thank God again and drive on, feeling good, glowing away. God then says to me, "You're welcome, now write it." And I say, "Okay, God, write what?" And He says, "Write it". And I nod my head not knowing what He means. And He says, "Tell her what she needs to know."

So here I am at the typewriter and I'm going to do my best to tell you what you need to know. Here you are, twenty-four years old, you've grown into a beautiful young woman, you're getting married in June and I'll be walking you down the aisle. But there are certain things a father has to tell his daughter to send her off ready and prepared for the road of life ahead.

Being a dad, see, just being a parent, really – I mean I've never been a mom so I'll tell it like a dad – is the biggest job in life and the most important because you bring another life into this world and the parent has the responsibility to grow that life with love, courage, sweat, and tears and make sure that child has the foundations to do the right thing or what I call, giving your kid a toolbox for survival.

Kids start out little, but before you know it they're grown up and gone. You're living proof of that, kiddo. You were a baby when you were born and now you're twenty-four, at the firm and getting married, so . . .

I've got some writing to do. God says so. But don't worry. I won't be long. I don't know that much. But I do know this . . .

If you laugh a lot

and you love a lot

life sure is good.

LOVE

The great
French Marshall Lyautey
once asked his gardener to plant a tree.
The gardener objected that the tree was
slow growing and would not reach
maturity for 100 years.
The Marshall replied,
"In that case, there is no time
to lose; plant it this afternoon."

JOHN FITZGERALD KENNEDY

LOVE

Love. Now there's a four-letter word! Do you know how many books and poems and letters and stories and songs have been written on love? I'll bet you could go online right now and punch that four-letter word right into your search engine and you'd probably get a gazillion entries just on the word "love". Well, maybe it wouldn't be a gazillion, I don't know how many, exactly, but I do know one thing it would be a lot. That's for sure, because ever since man could think and draw and write he's been thinking and drawing and writing about love.

See, love is like the farm, or more exactly, love is like a garden, because the seeds you plant are the plants you get. If you plant a corn seed, don't be expecting eggplant. See how that works? Same thing with love – if you plant a bitchy seed, don't be expecting a hug to be coming your way. See?

But if you really want to love right, then love like a dog. I know, you're probably scratching your head and saying, love like a dog? Looks like Dad's lost it. But think about it. When you come home from work after a long day at the firm, who's there at the door, wiggling and waggling with that tail flip-flopping away? Huh? Dog, that's who.

Yep. You could've been gone twelve hours, and before you left you yelled at him for doing his business in the house or just barking too much or whatever. But even after all that abuse and punishment and loneliness, Dog is there at the door, wiggling and waggling. See, dogs know unconditional love.

And you say, right, Dad, love is like a dog in a garden. But what about when the sun isn't shining and I don't have a dog? What about when it's pouring rain and I'm soaking wet and my boss is a jerk and RC and I are fighting (Editor's note: RC, that's her husband-to-be) and the kids are screaming (Editor's Note again: No kids yet) and the mortgage is due and I've got a migraine, too? Huh? What about then, Dad?

Well, you're right, kiddo, I never said life was easy just because dogs make it look easy. But I've always found that when skies are dark and tornadoes are assaulting my brain and life seems upside down – almost worthless, I find one thing, one little seed of love and hope to hold on to. For me, it's usually a picture of you, my little kiddo, and the love I have for you. The miracle of birth, the joy of little laughs and smiles and silly kid things. And now you growing up into a beautiful young woman – when I think of those things, my heart smiles and I just can't be down anymore. That picture of a dad loving his daughter works for me – every time.

Then I think about this part in the Bible where it says that God loves me more than I love my own child, and that blows me away. Here's my heart, already overflowing with all this "Dadlove", and then God loves you even more than that. Now *that's* a lot of love. You know, that Bible has some good stuff in it, you ought to read it sometime.

Love, love, love – love is all you need. Maybe the Beatles were right. There's a lot to be said about love, and I sure don't intend to try and say it all here, but I will say this . . .

Love your work – or find something else to do. If you don't, you'll be like the Exxon Valdez, spilling oil all over the place, and nobody's happy about that, least of all, you.

Love your kids – even when they're crying and whining. Don't love the whining, love the kid. Love will heal all.

Love your husband – even when he leaves dirty socks on the floor. Look at the love, not the dirty socks.

Love your God – He made this whole crazy wonderful universe and you. Just say, "Thanks, God," and He'll be real happy.

Love your self – if you don't love you, who will?

And just remember if you love

like a dog in a garden,

your tail will

wiggle

and

waggle

and you'll be

one happy puppy.

RESPECT

*Don't go around saying
the world owes you a living,
the world owes you nothing,
it was here first.*

MARK TWAIN

RESPECT

The Hopi Indians have just two laws: Don't go around hurting each other and try to understand things. Two laws. Pretty simple. The Bible has the Golden Rule, "Do unto others, as you would have them do unto you." Again, pretty simple. There must be something to this respect thing.

I'm not saying you don't know respect, don't misunderstand me. You're very respectful. In fact, if there was a magazine called RESPECT, we could put your picture right on the front cover, that's how respectful you are. I'm downright proud of you, kiddo. You are something special.

But back when you were a little kid, about two years old, you didn't know about respect. We were down on Fairfield Beach one sunny day, just having fun, playing in the sand, and you were filling up this bottle with sand. Instead of pouring it onto the pile you had in front of you, you poured it onto your friend's head, and she wasn't too happy. Now of course, you were only two and you didn't know any better. You were probably just checking things out to see if it was okay to pour sand into someone else's hair. That's how we learn.

Well, I was still learning what it was to be a dad and I didn't quite know what to do, but I first thought I should smack you right then and there. But I didn't do that. I had only been a dad for two years myself and you had never behaved disrespectfully like that before – probably those terrible two's people talk about – so I said to you, you couldn't do that you couldn't be disrespectful of people, or I would have to punish you. You, you just laughed that little kid laugh, filled up that bottle and poured that sand all over my head. And laughed.

I gave you a warning, but you just had to check and see if I really meant what I said. Well, I did. I picked you up, smacked your butt, and took you crying in my arms straight up to your room. I was talking nice but firm the whole time to you about how I loved you but didn't love disrespectful behavior and you had to learn a lesson. You just cried louder. It near about broke my heart. Sometimes it's tough being a Dad.

But I had to be strong and be a dad and do the right

thing and teach you the lessons you needed to know and right then, you needed to know about respect. I looked straight into those weeping little eyeballs and told you that you could come out when you learned to respect other people. You said you learned. I told you to think about it for a while and you cried louder still. I left you in your room to think about it and went back to the sunshine, and your cries followed me right down to the sand. My heart wept inside and I wondered if I was doing the right thing.

You must've cried for an hour – seemed like days to me – and you finally cried yourself to sleep. I don't think you were too happy about being in that room while I was out building sand castles and playing in the waves, but when you woke up you called out the window, "Dad, can I come out", and I asked you if you were going to respect other people and you said you would. And you did. From then on, you've always been respectful. I didn't know then, with your crying and my heart aching, if I was doing the right thing, but it seems like you turned out just fine.

Aretha Franklin sings a fine song called, "Respect", but I can't sing except in the shower and I can't do that right now because water would get all down in the typewriter and wreck the paper and everything, but I will tell you this . . .

Respect other people, even when they seem downright braindead stupid, because God made them, too.

Respect your parents, even when they make you want to scream. Parents can be weird, but they're still your parents.

Respect your husband, even when you don't agree with him. You picked him, so listen, love, and make things work.

And mainly, respect yourself. Because with self-respect you can handle misunderstanding, disappointment and despair.

See, God made a miracle when He made you. And that's God talking, not me, so you ought to be able to respect that.

FAITH AND BELIEF

The thing always happens that
you really believe in;
and
the belief in a thing
makes it happen.

FRANK LLOYD WRIGHT

FAITH AND BELIEF

I know you remember our first trip to Katahdin. You know how I know? Because your first year at Syracuse you wrote and told me you had a friend there who liked backpacking, too, and you stayed up one night telling camping stories and you told our Katahdin story. And now you're about to get married in the Tetons to a man who loves the mountains, too. That's how I know you remember Katahdin. I learned a lesson in faith there, and you learned a lesson in belief. That was some trip.

It started out normal with a twelve hour drive from Manhattan to the north most point of the Appalachin Trail in Maine and we camped that night at Roaring Brook at the base of the mountain. My faith didn't get tested till the next day.

The first leg was a six mile hike through woods and trees and rocks and streams, mainly level, not a steep climb, and I figured no big deal. Well, I figured wrong. I didn't realize that eight year olds don't usually take six mile hikes every day, but you informed me quite clearly that you weren't having fun. You were crying and wanting to stop and rest and we were only ten minutes into the hike. All I wanted was to take you to the mountain I had loved as a kid and let you share that experience but you wanted nothing of it. You were bored and cranky and downright ornery. I didn't know what to do. I thought about turning back, but somehow I laughed a lot and prayed in my head, asking for help and tried to show you the beauty of the wild mountain – and then we saw our first moose. I think Bullwinkle was God's answer to my call for help and it came just in the nick of time because I was running out of ideas and patience. But old Bullwinkle changed your mind about hiking and we made it into camp okay. You picked up sticks and I split some wood and we had ourselves a nice campfire and cooked dinner and told stories and watched shooting stars in that black Maine sky until you fell asleep. And I thanked God for helping me keep the faith and get through the tough times – and for sending Bullwinkle.

The next day was easy, just a little two-mile hike into Russell Pond. How easy was it? Well, it was so easy we were singing on the trail and two hours later we were at the pond fixing lunch. We made sandwiches, took a canoe out and had a picnic on the pond and admired the mighty mountain we were about to climb. Another Bullwinkle came by with her baby and they had lunch in the pond, too. They had seaweed and we had peanut butter and jelly. It was a good lunch on the pond, the big mountain reaching up to the sky with all God's creation everywhere and we were happy.

And then the ranger came back. I was wondering where she was because Russell Pond has a ranger station and you have to check in at each station, but she wasn't there when we arrived. Then she told us where she had been.

There was an accident on the mountain, up on the Knife's Edge. This teenager had taken a fall off the trail. (Editor's. Note: Did you ever look at the edge of a knife and see how skinny it is? And how it goes straight down on each side? Well, that's how they got the name for this trail.) This teenager fell and broke one arm and both legs and they had to have a helicopter come and airlift him out. The ranger lady is telling us all this and I'm watching you watching her, with your little kid eyes bugging right out of your head and I know what you're thinking because I can see it clear as day right there on your face. We thanked the ranger lady for telling us where she'd been and she went back to her ranger station.

Of course, I'm thinking in my mind that you must

be half scared out of your wits. Here's this teenager, broke both legs and an arm and you're only eight, so what's going to happen to you? Well, I told you how accidents happen and how when I was a kid hiking this mountain there were accidents but never with any of our campers because we were careful and had respect for the power of the mountain and if you stayed alert and paid attention and had respect, you didn't have accidents like that. And besides, teenagers can be stupid sometimes, too, and I'm sure that kid was probably horsing around when he should have been having respect for this mighty mountain. I told you all that and then some. You nodded your head and asked when are we going to eat?

We packed out at sun up the next day. It was going to be a long hike up and over the mountain and we would need all the daylight there was. My faith got tested again that day. Remember how heavy our packs were with food for six days, clothes, tent, and ax? Well, it was a steep climb from the start and the weight of your pack was too much for you and I took it and strapped it onto the back of my pack and we went on. But it just got steeper and steeper still until we were practically climbing straight up, grabbing saplings and tree roots so we wouldn't fall over backwards. And you started crying, right there while we were climbing and I started thinking, second-guessing in my mind, what have I done? Here we are out in the middle of nowhere on the backside of the mountain and we can't exactly take the TV remote and change channels. I should have thought about how difficult it would be for an eight year old, I should have planned better.

But there we were in the middle of the Maine wilderness and we had no choice. We had to climb on. So I told stories about boys twice your age who cried, too, because the mountain was so tough and I just kept saying over and over you can do it, you can do it, you can do it. You kept crying and we kept climbing and I kept wondering to myself, what did I get us into? And finally, tears and all, we cleared the tree line.

Remember that sight, kiddo? Remember how dense and thick and dark the forest was when we began and then how the trees started thinning out and getting smaller, almost like little dwarf trees – and then we broke into the light. Remember what it felt like when we cleared the tree line and looked back? Our tears turned to laughs. There was Russell Pond way down below and lakes and streams and valleys and mountains as far as the eye could see and we just laughed and cried and yelled at all this magnificence. We knew right there that we had won. We had climbed through the steep and the fear and the struggle and the doubt and the tears and the pain and we made it up into the light. We looked back over the darkness we had conquered and laughed – and then I looked at my watch.

High noon, broke camp at six, maybe eight hours of daylight left minus the mountain's shadow we were hiking into and we'd only come two miles with ten more to go. We had a quick lunch of granola bars and apples looking out over the world below, checked our map and moved on. We didn't want darkness catching us up on the mountain.

We hiked like mountain goats the rest of the day, sure-footed and light over rocks and streams. We were in the light. We had conquered the mighty mountain. We were winners, walking with the gods at the top of Mount Olympus. Darkness actually did catch us that last quarter mile coming into camp, but it didn't bother us. We just pulled out our flashlights and hiked in the dark. We were winners. Katahdin was ours.

The ranger was relieved when we pulled into Chimney Pond. They were just getting ready to send out a search party. Katahdin, see, is one powerful mountain, you check into and out of campsites so the rangers can track you and make sure that every climbing party is accounted for at the end of the day. So, Ranger Rick was happy to see us and we had the best dinner ever that night, chicken noodle soup and macaroni and cheese. It's funny, kiddo, how food always tastes better after you've conquered the world. We laughed and talked and even after we turned out our flashlights we kept talking and laughing and I finally said we had to go to sleep because tomorrow we were going to the peak – and we laughed some more. Victory is sweet.

The hike to the peak was a simple three mile loop. While I was cleaning up the breakfast dishes, you went up to the ranger station to check things out. We took a day pack with fiber bars and fruit and cookies, filled our canteens and hit the trail. Passing the ranger station you asked, "Dad, what trails are we taking", and I told you we were going up the Cathedral, across the Knife's Edge and down Dudley, and you said oh. Now that trail to the base of the Cathedral was only a five minute walk from Chimney, but you wanted to stop every thirty seconds because you were tired. I was getting pretty frustrated by the tenth stop and it finally dawned on me to ask, "Are you afraid?" You said you were because the signs at the ranger station said no one under the age of nine should climb the Cathedral or the

Knife's Edge or Dudley, and there we were getting ready to do exactly that. Boy, was I relieved.

See, I knew about fear and doubt and what they can do to a person, but I also knew about faith and belief and what they can do, so I just told you what I knew. I said, well, I can understand, kiddo, I was afraid the first time I climbed to the peak and I was thirteen, but here's what I found out about fear. If you do anything with fear you get into trouble, like that teenager that fell off, but yesterday I saw you, eight years old, hike twelve miles in thirteen hours up and over that mountain and I totally believe you can go to the top if you want to. But it's not up to what I believe, it's up to what you believe. We don't have to go to the peak, we can stay down here and check out the caves or just chill out. But if you want to go to the top, you can if you believe you can but that's your decision. That's what I said. And I looked at you and you looked at me and we just looked at each other. And then you said, let's go. You believed.

And go we did.

There's a reason they call that trail the Cathedral. Remember how big those rocks were, some bigger than cars, some bigger than pickup trucks, some bigger than a house, big rocks that glacier left, remember? But they didn't stop you, you were a little mountain goat, filled with belief – no fear, no doubt. You were going to the top.

I still keep that picture in my wallet, eight year old you, bony little knees, skinny little legs standing proud with your hands on your hips and Chimney Pond two thousand feet below and the whole world spreading out beyond, my kid at the top of the world. But then again, I'm just a proud dad.

Then we took the Knife's Edge. Oh yeah, fear came rushing back at us, a sixty-mile-an-hour gust will do that to you when you're on a trail eighteen inches wide that drops off on both sides a thousand feet or two. But we held tight to each other and the rocks and our belief and we didn't let go and we won again. We were so proud, victors of the mighty Katahdin.

And remember when we were driving away, we stopped and put the camera on the roof of the car and took a picture of us arm in arm with our fists raised and Mt. Katahdin behind us in the distance. Now you tell me, was the struggle worth it?

Thousands of books have been written on faith and belief and I can't cover it all here, but I will tell you this . . .

Believe in yourself. Even when the forest is dark and the climb is steep, keep on, keep the faith. You will always win – eventually – if you believe.

Believe in your husband. The tide is high and the tide is low. The sun comes up and the sun goes down. Don't doubt him in times of low tide and darkness. Keep the faith.

Believe in God. Let the storm clouds circle, you have a Friend. Keep on, keep the faith.

And believe in your Dad.

Because I said so.

SEX

After ecstasy,
the laundry.

ZEN PROVERB

SEX

Everybody always talks about four-letter words, but what about three-letter words like cat, dog or log? Actually, I'm thinking about two tough ones – God and sex. So I'm going to talk about sex now, but God will come into it, too. He made us and sex is part of the way He made us so you can't really talk about sex – or for that matter, life or death or love or hate or joy or sorrow – without God coming up.

Kids are always so curious and you were a kid once and you were curious, too. You were about five and you asked where babies came from and I told you a little bit about the love between a mom and a dad and how babies were born out of love and then come out of their mom's tummy. But the first time we ever talked about sex in a grown-up way you were ten.

We were up on the farm in North Ontario. I was out splitting wood and you got back from town. I asked you about town and you said it was fine, but you had an accident. You were in this store and all of a sudden you felt a little funny inside and went to the bathroom and that was when you discovered your first period. It was so normal to you that I just acted like it was normal to me and we talked a little about how God made you and how your body worked and whether it was better to use a tampon or a pad and how you were becoming a woman. You just said yeah, "Can I go play now," and off you went to play with your cousins. And I just sat there being a proud dad because of how you handled everything so mature – not bad, for ten years old. But kids are like that, life is just a natural flow and you deal with things as they happen, no big deal.

And then we grow up and we forget how to go with the natural flow. Grown-ups have a hard time talking about sex even though it's always on their minds. It seems to me that the way God made us, sex is the highest form of communication between two people who love and respect each other, not like those TV soap operas where everybody's sleeping with everybody else.

When you were thirteen, I tried to tell you how God made a sacred temple when He made the human being, body, heart and soul. But you said you already knew all about it, that sex was like baseball, first base, second base, third base, home, that's what everybody said. So I made you explain the bases to me and you actually did pretty good.

And I said, "You'll be dating and stuff and going out with different guys and they'll all be looking to hit home runs but there's more to baseball than hitting home runs. In my opinion, home runs are something special and reserved for marriage. Before that, you can explore first base and maybe second and there's a lot of exploring to explore just in kissing and, anyway, I didn't hit any home runs until I married your Mom and then I hit one out of the park and we got you."

That's all fine and good but that was then and this is now and now you're getting married. I don't want to know how long you've been hitting home runs or when you hit your first, but you've got a whole lifetime ahead of you and sex and God will always be a part of that life and the biggest mistake most people make is they don't talk about sex or God because it's just too difficult or embarrassing. But I've got to tell you because God told me to tell you, so here goes . . .

Sex is like a violin. In the wrong hands it can be harsh and shrill but in the right hands there will be excitement, elation and ecstasy. See, it's how you tune it and hold it and touch it and play it. It takes time and lots of practice to be a great violinist. Take the time. Practice a lot. It's worth it.

Sex is talking. Two people up close and personal and talking with their hearts and minds and bodies instead of just talking words. The other side of talking is listening, so talk and listen with love and trust and you ought to have a pretty good time.

Sex is pleasing your husband. And vice versa. Give and you shall receive. There's God's law again. Be generous, be gentle, be curious, have fun. And be sure and tell each other what you like – massage, touch here, kiss there. RC can please you if you tell him what you like. And vice versa, too. See how that works?

Sex is like medicine. You will face struggles and challenges, mountains of life to climb, but when two people love each other they can help each other through the bad times and some of the best medicine for bad and good is making love.

Sex is good. God talks about it in Proverbs. In India they have the Kama Sutra. Vietnamese lore says that sex is the cure for whatever ails you – common cold, migraine, bad moods. Modern studies show that couples who make love more frequently are healthier, have fewer heart attacks and live longer and happier lives.

And one final warning: Never, never, never use

sex against each other or to punish each other. That's taking love and using it for something bad. God doesn't like that and a whole lot of ugly nasties will get you instead of all the good God intended.

So, if sex is like baseball, just remember that a game takes nine innings, sometimes extra innings. And it's more than just a single or a double or a homer, it's a whole bunch of different plays and moves and strategies all strung together. And what's really cool is, if you play it right, you both get to win.

Live longer.

Be happier.

Enjoy.

PRAY AND PLAY

Never let your head hang down. Never give up and sit and grieve. Find another way. And don't pray when it rains if you don't pray when the sun shines.

SATCHEL PAIGE

PRAY AND PLAY

Remember Christmas of '96 when we were out in L.A. at your Uncle Tim's and we were buying presents, books more exactly. You know I've been giving books for Christmas the past five years because they last forever, never go out of style and some of them are even pretty good. I had twelve or thirteen in my arms and they were all about God and spiritual and inspirational stuff and you said dad, not everybody's as spiritual as you. Well, I was just laughing to myself because you're probably right.

I guess growing up on the farm taught me the miracle of life early. To this day, I'm still amazed like a kid in a dinosaur museum when spring rolls around and black naked trees burst forth with leaves overnight and the bare earth sends up flowers and buds of every color imaginable. It's a miracle to me. So I just pray every morning and give thanks that I'm alive for one more day, one more chance and I pray every night and give thanks for my wonderful life, my cherished family and friends and my extra-special super wonderful kid. And I go to sleep smiling.

Here's how I see it. You can pray or not pray.

Maybe you say how do I know there really is a God? Or if there is a God, how come there's so much crime and murder and wars and poverty? And hurricanes and floods and tornadoes and divorce and starvation? Huh, dad, what about all that? And what about . . .

Well, now. Listen, here little miss whippersnapper, and I'll try and answer you. People have been asking those same questions for thousands of years and philosophers and scientists have been theorizing and testing and guessing about just as long and they're still looking for the answers. The only thing that I can figure out is that life is a mystery.

I know what you're thinking. That's pretty simplistic, dad, but check it out. What does the Bible say? What about the Buddhists, the Muslims, the American Indians, the Zen masters, the Tao? Check it out. I've been asking the same questions myself the last thirty years and reading books and best as I can tell, it all comes down to what you choose to believe – God or no God.

See, it's funny, but everything happens for a reason, and God knows the reason even when we don't. That's one thing I pray for every day, understanding – to better know the mysteries of life and the intricacies of other people because it turns out, much to my surprise, that not everybody thinks like I do.

Look at the Egyptians, living on the Nile. Every year the river swelled up over the banks and flooded the land. Now usually we think a flood is a bad thing, but the Egyptians understood that the flood actually re-fertilized the valley and their tomatoes grew bigger than anybody else's. So for the Egyptians, flood was good, not bad, because flood made for better tomatoes. Be like an Egyptian – see the good in things instead of always looking for the bad.

Still skeptical? That's okay. I can understand. So was I, but how about a not so philosophical or spiritual approach. Did you read "Catcher in the Rye"? Holden Caufield said his prayers every night just in case there was a God. That made sense to me as a teenager and helped me get through the times of doubt and confusion. Maybe that'll help you, too, if you need it. So say your prayers every night – just in case there is a God.

Now you're probably wondering, why pray and play, Dad? Well because just like sex and God, pray and play are real close and go hand in hand. Look. When I'm struggling or fussing or fighting or whining, I'm usually in a foul mood and not thinking about God at all. Or if

I am thinking about God, it's usually like why are you so mean, God, making me go through this ugly, painful self-pity, woe is me, blah blah stuff? But when I'm playing, I'm laughing and light-hearted and loving life and I feel close to God, and then I'm praying and playing and giving thanks for all the good things in my life.

Best as I can figure out, kiddo, praying is like talking to your best friend. Only difference is, when God is your best friend, then you're playing with the greatest power in the universe. And when you're playing with the creative power of the universe on your side, there's a pretty good chance that you will come out winning. Will there be failure and loss? A lot. Pain? Too much. Death? Inevitable.

So does that mean just because times are tough you stop believing and give up? No, that means there's high tide, there's low tide; sun up, sun down; breathe in, breathe out. That's life. Now all you have to do is decide, God or no God?

Why do the good and the bad always seem to come together? You can't see the stars 'til the sky gets dark, that's just the way it is. Why can't you just have all good? I don't know, it'd probably be boring, but best I can figure, it's a little like spoiling a child.

If you just give kids anything they want without guidance and without them having to work for it or earn it or deserve it, what usually happens to the kid, ever notice? Seems to me most spoiled kids are out of control and they don't respect others, themselves, their parents, nothing. They're whining in supermarkets, disrespectful and talking back to parents in restaurants. The parents aren't taking charge and the kids are out of control. It isn't right that the parents don't teach their kids the Golden Rule. Everybody gets hurt when the parents don't do their job – the kids, the families, the parents, the community, society, everybody – just because the parents don't have time to do the right thing. Well, that's a lousy excuse. Parents have to make the time to do the right thing because they're the parents. Period.

I know, you're saying fine, Dad, but what do spoiled kids in supermarkets have to do with praying and playing? Well, I'm just about to tell you.

See, it isn't the kids fault, it's the parents. Kids don't know inherently what's right or wrong, but they want to know. They want to know really badly and they're always looking for guidance and answers and who do they look to first but their parents. But what happens when the parents don't have time – or worse yet –

don't know the difference between right and wrong because they're reading tabloid psycho papers and watching TV? Now you can find wisdom and knowledge just about anywhere if you know where to look, but TV and tabloids would not be my number one choice. No, today both Mom and Dad are working trying to make ends meet and the kids are at daycare being raised by strangers and things go out of control because there's no guidance in the family. Well how about this for a brilliant idea, why not play and pray with your kids?

See, just talk to God and ask for guidance and wisdom. If He made the whole universe and planets and stars and sun and moon and plants and animals and humans, too, He probably knows what to do about teaching your children and doing the right thing, but you have to ask Him. Seek and ye shall find. Ask and it shall be given unto you. Knock and the door shall be opened. God is just waiting to open the door and tell you all He knows. So pray and play and kids won't be brats and life won't be so confusing. Pray and play, that's what I say.

Like when we went to hike the Grand Canyon and we stood there on the South rim for the first time and looked out over one of the Seven Wonders of the

World and I said, "Kiddo, look at what God made," and you said, "Wow," and we both just nodded our heads in amazement. We were praying. And then we camped in that canyon by the river and hiked the desert floor by the light of the full moon. We were playing.

Or like when we were standing at the edge of the mighty Niagara and that wall of water must have been at least a foot thick, maybe two, and I said, "Kiddo, look at that," and we both just nodded our heads, knowing the incredible force of life right then and there. We were praying. Then we took the Maid of the Mists to get closer to the force and we were playing.

Or like that Thanksgiving up on the farm, I think you were eleven. There we were, out in the bush, no electricity, no running water, just a bucket and a well, and the sauna for bathing, just having fun and loving life. The snow began to fall late Saturday afternoon and we just prayed for it to keep on falling so we could stay up on the farm another day or two, fire up the sauna, roll in the snow and keep on playing. Our prayers were answered again and we got to stay and play another day.

That's why I say, pray and play. Celebrate life, give thanks to the Great Spirit every day because we have been truly blessed. When you look at all the life we've lived and the fun we've had and the places we've been and seen, you know there's goodness in this world. What can you say except, "thanks".

It seems to me that if you look around, most people don't pray and play and they end up living lonely lives of silent desperation, and that's fine if that's how you choose to live your life. But then look at what we've done your first twenty-four years, and I'd have to say that praying and playing is working out pretty good, but that's just my opinion.

I'm proud of you, kiddo, seeing how you've done, growing up, becoming a woman, making decisions, doing the right thing – real proud.

So, I just
pray
and play
and say,
thank you,
God
for this
wonderful
kid.

TRUST AND MARRIAGE

If you build castles in the air,
your work need not be lost;
that is where they should be.
Now put foundations under them.

HENRY DAVID THOREAU

TRUST AND MARRIAGE

Back when your Mom and I got married, way back in 1970, they didn't have pre-nuptial agreements about who gets the car or the house or the dog when you get divorced. What kind of commitment is that, anyway? That's saying I don't trust that our marriage will work out and I don't trust you so let's divide things up ahead of time so there won't be fighting over the dog when we split up. To me, that is a very strange way to begin a lifetime commitment.

But then who am I to talk about marriage? I'm divorced. Well, I'm your Dad, that's who I am, and I may have failed as a husband the first time out, but I didn't fail as a Dad. And if you want to talk about divorce, we can talk about divorce, but let me tell you something right up front, I never heard of a good divorce and I speak with first-hand experience. But right now, I'm talking about trust and marriage, and divorce is not an option.

You were born out of love between your mom and me and then we got divorced. Somehow you survived. Together, Dad and kid, we cried our tears and patched our hearts and lived in light and love and in spite of the hurt and the pain, you turned out pretty good. I think there might be a lesson in that, finding the love and letting go of the sadness. And since I'm your Dad, I'm going to tell you what you need to know about trust and marriage. So there.

It's funny how we always make such a big deal out of failure, when failure and making mistakes is just part of how we learn. Go and ask Thomas Edison how many times he failed to get the light bulb right and he'll tell you how many ways not to make a light bulb. And the truth be known, I've probably made as many mistakes as old "Tom Ed", maybe more, and maybe that just means I've learned a little more than the average Dad. But then again, maybe not.

Either way, I've had a lot of fun so far, failures and all, and you've turned out okay, failures and all, and I am your Dad, failures and all, so I will tell you about trust and marriage, failures and all.

See, marriage is a lifetime commitment, "till death do us part". This is serious stuff because till death is a pretty long time and it will take some serious commitment to each other to meet all of life's challenges and changes separately together. It will take a lot of listening and patience and understanding and forgiveness and mainly – a lot of love.

Most times it seems like people go through life without a plan. Only problem is, if you don't know where you're going then that's exactly where you'll end up. That would be like taking a six-day hike with no map, no compass, no menu, no matches, no food, no tent, no plan – and "till death do us part" is a little longer than a six-day hike. Would you take a vacation for two weeks without knowing where you were going? So then why would you head out on a lifetime journey without some kind of plan?

First off, you need to get your priorities straight. Most times, people get started in adult life with a job, and a job is good because you get paid and you need money to pay bills in adult life. Ideally, you really want to own your own business so you can be in control of your life, because with a job, you also get a boss, and the boss is in charge. And the boss will tell you what time to wake up and what to wear to work and what time you can get hungry for lunch and what time to go home and how much time you get each year for vacation.

So now you've made a commitment to your husband and your boss, and what happens if they both need you at the same time? Which one comes first? That's a priority question, and I say your husband takes priority over the job. See, jobs'll change and bosses'll change, but your commitment to your husband is for a lifetime.

But people tend to get caught up in the rat race. What a picture, a bunch of furry, long-tailed vermin racing around the track, no plan, no priorities, just survival. There's a lot of people out there just surviving and they think that's fine, but I'm your Dad and I didn't raise you to be a rat. Do good at your job, yes. Give a hundred percent, yes. But when push comes to shove, take time for your husband. Show RC you're thinking about him. Put a little love note in his briefcase, so when he opens it up for his big, important meeting he'll see your note and remember the good things in life – and his meeting will go better, too. Little things can make a big difference, and how do you keep a lifetime commitment anyway? One day at a time.

Now you've got your commitment to your husband and your commitment to your job/boss. Then somewhere down the line, let's say you add kids. Well, kids need diapers changed and dinner made and rides to practice and now you've got all these balls in the air and you didn't even study juggling in college. Now what do you do?

Well, here again, you've got to have a plan and have your priorities straight. You can look around and see most people don't have a plan. They think they're firefighters; run over here put a fire out, run over there put a fire out, juggling balls and fighting fires. But kids need a whole lot of love and time and attention and direction and how do you handle it all? Priorities.

Just remember, kids start out little and then grow up and leave. You have them for eighteen years or so and then they're gone. Kids come and go, jobs come and go, but you and RC are still there. So it's RC, then kids, then job when it comes to priorities. Work the other stuff out around the commitment to your marriage and each other first.

But how do you handle all the balls to juggle and the fires to fight and the rats to race? Well, you can do like most people, watch trash TV or listen to radio talk show gurus or take anti-depressants or read the latest hip-hop pop new age psychology or check your horoscope or get your palm read or see a shrink or have another martini. Or you can turn it all off, be quiet and talk to God. Yes, here comes God again. He's everywhere, He's everywhere.

Here's how I see it. The more I live and the more I laugh and the more I love and the more I listen and the more I look, there's God. Life is so helter-skelter, fast-paced today that you've got to have a solid foundation in your life just to weather all the storms.

See, marriage is kind of like a house. What kind of house will you build if you don't have a plan? Which comes first, the frame or the sheet rock, the wiring or the plumbing, the roof or the floor? And then if you build your house without a foundation, what's going to happen when the first big storm comes rolling in? It's like the three little pigs and the big, bad wolf – which house withstood the wolf?

Now, you and RC are building a life together. I know it will be a wonderful life. I believe in you both. You want to build your house of marriage on a solid foundation, so I say build on the rock of God, Creator of all the universe.

So as far as priorities go, put God first, then husband/wife, then kids, then business/career. That's how it looks to me. Rats in the race might see things differently, but you have to ask yourself, do you really want to be just another rat?

Trust God first. He made you – your heart to feel,

your mind to think, your eyes to look, your nose to smell, your fingers to touch, your ears to hear, the birds, the bees, the flowers, the trees. He had a plan then and He still has a plan today.

The racing rats will say you can get free condoms in school but you can't say prayers because someone might get offended. But I say the rats are wrong. You can see it in their brat rat kids and their rathole homes and their beady little rat eyes. Rats are fine, there's a place for rats in this world, otherwise God wouldn't have made them, but I'm your Dad, and I didn't raise a rat.

So trust in God. And trust your husband. And tell him I said he should trust in you, too. And leave the rats to their racing. You've got other things to do.

Honor your commitment,

trust each other,

listen,

respect,

laugh,

love,

pray,

play,

take time for

the little things.

Believe in

God,

each other,

your commitment

–

and keep the faith.

Because I said so

and I'm your Dad.

DIVORCE AND FORGIVENESS

Write injuries in dust,
benefits in marble.

BENJAMIN FRANKLIN

DIVORCE AND FORGIVENESS

Remember that summer when you and RC came to New York and I picked you up at Penn Station? It was late, around eleven, and that was my first time meeting RC. We took pictures with Madison Square Garden in the background and another with this big KOOL billboard in the background because you kids are so cool. I figured you'd be hungry, want to get something to drink, do a little tour of the Big Apple, but you said you were tired and wanted to check in so I drove you up to the hotel. The whole time I'm thinking in my mind while we we're making small talk, "The Pierre. That's a ritzy hotel, even more so than the Plaza. The firm must have a corporate suite or something and the kids were able to book it for the weekend. Sharp kids."

You two went and checked in while I waited on the street. Five minutes, ten minutes, fifteen minutes, and I'm scratching my head, thinking it's taking awfully long for you kids to check in. And finally after twenty minutes you two come out, arm in arm, smiling, and before I could say a thing you said, "Dad, we've got to tell you something". I said, "Sure, sweetie, what's up?" You stuck your hand out to show me your ring and said, "We're engaged." We hugged and laughed and cried and hugged and laughed and hooted and hollered right there on Fifth Avenue.

Nobody was tired anymore. We all piled into the front seat of my car laughing, hugging, snapping pictures. We stopped at Rockefeller Plaza, piled out and took pictures; then Times Square, piled out, more pictures; then to our old loft on 43rd and 7th, piled out, more pictures again; and finally off to the World Trade Center on the last elevator up to the 107th floor for champagne toasts – and more pictures.

We called your Bubbie from there to tell her the good news, and RC told us how he had the ring in his pocket all day long, touching it, feeling it, giving into anticipation, waiting for the right time to pop the question. I was just honored and touched that you two took the time in this crazy mixed up world to think of your Dad. Thanks. It meant a lot to me.

We talked about life and love and commitment and communication and raised our champagne with toast after toast. We had the waitress take our picture. And I just kept thinking in my mind, mark one up for love.

See, kiddo, you're a survivor. Yep. You're a survivor of the holocaust of divorce. You're actually more than just a survivor – way more. Not only did you survive, but you found love and forgiveness in your heart even as the dark storms were tearing up your little three-year old life. You are amazing. How did you do that?

There I was, "the Dad" and I had all this hurt and pain and sadness in my heart about splitting up with your Mom, guilt and confusion swirling in my brain. I take full responsibility for my part in that divorce. We all make our own beds and then we have to sleep in them. And there you were. You didn't ask to be there. You had nothing to do with the divorce.

We could have gotten lost and eaten up by the pain and the darkness, casualties of divorce, but we looked for the love instead of dwelling on the dark. There's all this natural love a Dad has for his daughter and the same kind of love a daughter has for a Dad. We chose to focus on that love. All the confusion was between the grown-ups. Your Mom always loved you. I always loved you. The adult mess had nothing to do with you.

Was it tough? Yes. Was it sad? Uh-huh. Were there tears? Plenty. We got lucky and booked ourselves tickets on the love boat of life. We rode out the choppy seas and violent storms and found our way to the sunlight. And you know why this was? Because of you.

You were just a little child of God, full of love and forgiveness. Your love and forgiveness was an example to me. That's why when you and RC came to New York to tell me about your engagement, I said to myself, "mark one up for love," because love won again. Life is love and light versus darkness and hate and love won in your life. Thanks, kiddo, for all your love and forgiveness.

Divorce is very popular today. In 1998, twenty million people in America, maybe more, were divorced. And how many more get divorced each year? Just because something's popular doesn't mean it's the right thing to do. I never heard of a good divorce. There are a lot of people out there today fussing and fighting, kicking and biting, and a lot of kids that get caught up in that battle and a lot of lives that get smashed on the rocks of divorce. And unfortunately, there are a lot of people that never recover – or should I say never choose to recover. All of life is a choice.

And we chose love over hate and forgiveness and moving on over stagnating in the stench of resentment. Remember how life is like a garden, you get what you plant? So what do you want growing in the garden of your life, brambles and thorns or flowers and fruit? Plant hate and you'll get weeds enough to strangle every living thing in your life. But plant love and anything is possible.

Buddha tells this story about hiking a mountain path with a young monk. They come upon an old woman by a stream who needs help to get across. Buddha puts her on his back and carries her to the other side. He and the young monk hike on. Hours later they stop to rest and the young monk asks the Great One, does he feel guilty for touching the woman and violating his vow of celibacy. Buddha says, we have come many miles. I helped another soul and left her at the stream. Why do you still carry her?

It's like what Thoreau or Emerson or one of those New England writers said, "Change what you can change and accept what you can't change." There's no sense fussing about something you can't change. All the fussing in the world won't change it, so move on.

See, kiddo, if the truth be known, I'm not perfect. I know that may come as shock to you, but it's the truth. Nobody's perfect except for God; not you, not RC, not your Mom, not me. That's just the way it is.

And I figure if God forgives all my mistakes and still loves me, and you forgive my mistakes and still love me, then I might as well forgive myself and move on, learn and grow, love and forgive.

Thanks for all your love and forgiveness, kiddo.

Listen to me.

I'm your Dad.

Do as I say,

not as I do.

Divorce

is not

an option.

TALK, LAUGH AND LISTEN

We live very close together. So our prime purpose in life is to help others. And if you can't help them, at least don't hurt them.

THE DALI LAMA

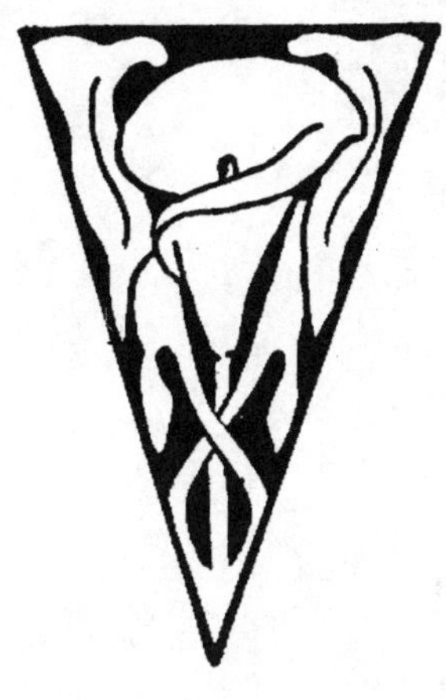

TALK, LAUGH AND LISTEN

Remember how the Hopi have two laws? Well, Dad's got two laws, too. Here they are, Dad's Two Laws of Communication; 1) Got a problem, take a walk, and 2) If you don't have something nice to say, shut up.

Okay, they're not really laws and they're not really mine but they are appropriate bits of wisdom that have come down through the ages on how to talk and not talk to one another. You would think that talking is easy, just open your mouth and move your lips and the words come out and you're talking. Easy. But then something weird happens like some invisible force that changes your words in mid-air so that the person who hears them hears something totally different than what you said or you thought you said. If you've ever had a lovers' quarrel you know what I mean. Words get confused and misunderstood and messed up real quick and before you know it there's hurt feelings and defensiveness and anger and revenge and all of a sudden talking isn't so easy anymore.

Best as I can tell we're all different. We hear things differently. Feel differently. Listen differently. Think differently. Man, woman, black, white, liberal, conservative, Christian, Jew, Greek, Irish – all different. Sometimes I'm amazed we haven't killed each other off already. History proves that we sure have been trying really hard since the beginning of time.

Then look at kids. Kids don't have that problem. Kids don't care if you're black or Jew or conservative or white as long as you'll play with them. And when they do fight and pick on each other it's without regard to race, color or creed. They just beat each other up, get over it, kiss and make up and keep on playing.

But when we become grown-ups we get clever and smart and know everything. We're so cultivated, sophisticated, so worldly-wise and we learn how to hold grudges and seek revenge and get even tit for tat so there and sometimes we'll hold grudges for days and weeks and months and years – look at the Greeks and

Turks and British and Irish and Arabs and Jews. Sometimes talking is a little tougher than it looks, unless you're a kid.

But now you're a grown-up, getting married and you and RC are making a lifetime commitment to each other and I know you know all about love and forgiveness and trust and respect and faith and belief, but I'm talking about talking because talking can be tough, especially when you don't listen.

If you don't listen you can't hear and if you don't hear you can't understand and if you don't understand then you're confused, and communication breaks down. "Houston, we've got a problem." So take a walk. Get a little air on the brain.

See, what usually happens when we talk is that each person has his own point of view which comes from experience or something Dad said or Mom said or a friend said or a teacher said or a preacher said or a stranger said or a TV starlet said and we take it on to be our own personal point of view and we take a stand in our minds because we believe we're right and now we have to make a point.

Well, that's fine and good if you're in a debate but marriage is not a debate, it's not about winning points or being persuasive or being right, it's about understanding and compassion. You win points in marriage by being a good listener, not proving points and being right.

I speak with abundant knowledge and first-hand experience. I was a know-it-all; bright, smart, Greek, opinionated, stubborn, and bull-headed (not to mention quick-tempered and a lousy listener). Fortunately, God made us with freedom of choice so we can change, and I've learned a lot in this wonderful life and have grown and changed. Now it's my responsibility as your father to pass it on. I hope it helps.

In the past I wasn't a very good listener because I thought I was always right. When you're always right you don't have to listen, all you have to do is make your point and be right. But that usually turns into a disagreement, fight, hurt feelings, name calling, yelling, tears. Not a pretty picture. I could probably write a book on how not to communicate.

Hurt feelings, wounded hearts, feeling like a jerk, not liking myself – that was me. I can tell you first-hand how not to make things work. But I'm learning and growing and changing, hopefully into a better person. Now if I don't have something nice to say I don't say it, and that works much better than being right and I feel good about myself for keeping my mouth shut.

And even though I might have been a jerk I always knew how to talk to kids and be a good father. We hiked and camped and skied and golfed and played bridge and cooked and sang and laughed and listened, and now you and RC are getting ready to get married and you kids like to do the same things you did as a kid, so I must have done something right. Yes, kiddo, you are ready for marriage. You are prepared and I know that the joy we've shared together will be a part of you forever.

You're heading out on the road of life, your own road, together with your man, your partner for life. You will make your own plans and hike your own mountains and follow your own dreams together. I'm excited. The short time we've had together – you, RC and me – I see how you play together and cook together and work together and respect each other and care for each other. The journey lies ahead, the adventure of life is yours. You will do great.

There will be clear sailing and there will be dangerous curves ahead, detours, roads under construction, accidents, rush hour traffic, potholes, missed exits, flat tires and more clear sailing. That's life. And that's why you have to learn to laugh – a lot.

When you find yourself stuck in that rush hour traffic, just remember that you have a choice. You can get stressed out and upset or you can laugh. Think about it. Will all the stress in the world make the traffic go away? But laughing will make you feel better and you can't control the traffic but you can control how you react to it. The scientific community has even done studies on the healthy aspects of laughing. In fact, Norman Cousins, famous magazine editor, actually rid his body of cancer through laughing. So laugh. Ha ha.

Remember how life is like a garden? Well, your words are seeds. Whatever you say will fall in the ground and grow. Think about it. What will you get in your garden if you blame, criticize, find fault, whine, and complain? You have to ask yourself, do *you* really want those plants in the garden of *your* life? Think before you talk – what kind of garden do you want?

And before you think, take a deep breath, talk to God and ask for guidance and understanding. Then, if you've got something nice to say, go for it. If not, shut up and take a walk and talk to God some more and let go of the anger and keep on walking until you can find something good to say.

Be a Hopi; try and understand things. Every problem has a solution so just take the time to find it – then do the right thing. Make it work. You can do it.

And if all else fails, go talk to the dog in the garden. Dogs are good listeners and they don't talk back.

FAMILY AND FRIENDS

Don't forget this. You are an essential piece
of the puzzle of humanity...
Once you know who you are and to whom you are linked,
you will know what to do.

EPICTETUS 81A.D.

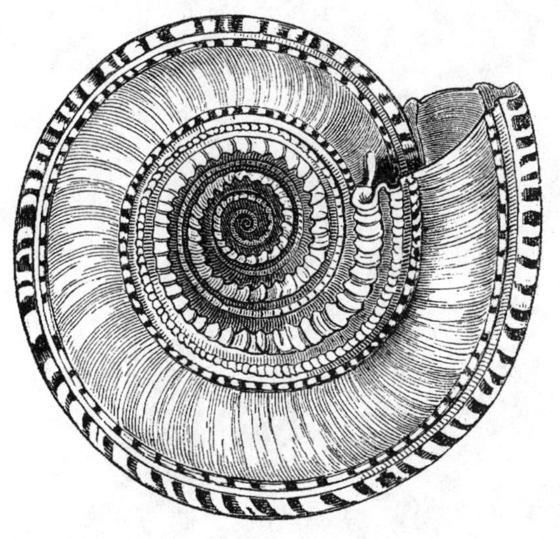

FAMILY AND FRIENDS

My how time flies. It won't be long till I'll be walking you down the aisle to send you off on your journey of life and it seems only like yesterday that you were born. March 24th, 1974 at 11:42 in the morning you came into this world. I'll never forget that moment, your squooshed little head and skinny little arms and teeny tiny little fingers all wiggling and reaching for life in this strange new world. Wow! If you don't believe in God just go and have a baby and be there for the birth, and experience the miracle of life and then tell me you don't believe in God. And now you're getting married.

I'm standing over this box of pictures, thousands of them, and flipping through the last twenty-four years and I'm just smiling ear-to-ear. My heart is full. I am one proud Dad. We've lived life and shared many lessons and I totally believe that you are prepared to enter your marriage with a good head, a strong heart and a wise young soul.

You know how I know? Because I'm your Dad, that's how. Looking at all these pictures and memories and moments, and all the places we've been and mountains we've climbed, and sand castles we've built, and people we've met, and things we've done and seen, and our family and friends. What a life! Every picture tells a story.

See, kiddo, we've been blessed. Somehow through all the troubles and challenges and potholes of life and living and growing up, we knew that with love and family and friends we could weather any storm. Darkness came, bad things happened, tragedy struck, confusion and misunderstanding swirled, sadness made our hearts heavy, death took Papou away and we're still standing and smiling and ready for more. And that's how I know you're ready to get married.

I'm putting all these pictures together for you in a little family scrapbook, a picture book of your first twenty-four years of life with Dad so you can remember – as if you need it – all the good times we've had and the lessons we've learned and the love we've shared with family and friends. And no one or no thing can ever take that away from you. You lived it first-hand and it's in your heart and in your soul and you stand strong with the love of family and friends.

There's Uncle Dimitri and you and me at Bell Rock in Sedona just laughing and goofing around. D always keeps us laughing whether we're walking the dog or learning about the ancient Anasazi medicine wheel. He should be a comedian.

And there's Uncle Steve, the one-armed wonder of the Great White North, wiser than his years. Even though that cable and winch took his left arm, it didn't take his heart and he's still hammering nails and building homes and raising kids and today he helps other injured people all across Canada to pick up and go on and make the best of their lives. He's a special man.

And there's Aunt Susanna, scouting sea lions on the California coast with her heart so big and her smile so warm and she, too, has dedicated her life to helping others with her strong spirit and her can-do attitude. She's a saint.

And there's your Uncle Tim and your cousin Heather sneaking up on Bubbie at the Atlanta airport to give her a surprise for Christmas. Tim is such an inspiration. He was a teenage junkie but turned his life around and today he's the wonderful dad of three beautiful daughters.

And there's Papou, weakened from his stroke, but still strong and proud as ever showing you mementos from his flight group in the Second World War. I remember how proud he was when you were born. You were the first grandchild and you must have been ten days old at the time, and we took you in to the restaurant. Papou took little baby you all around the whole restaurant so everyone could meet you; customers at tables, chefs in the kitchen, waitresses, busboys, everybody. And when he was done with the tour he took a bus tray – clean, of course – and lined it with tablecloths and made a bassinet right there beside our table. And how he loved to play bridge with you. Papou was such a big teaser.

And there's you and Bubbie in the Arizona sunset with pink and purple clouds radiating from your heads, looking like angels in the sky. She is so proud of you. You've meant so much to her since Papou died. See, death took Papou after forty-seven years of life together and Bubbie was left alone with only her memories. It was pretty dark and sad for her but you always called her and wrote little notes and cheered her up and you reminded her of the love of family. She's healing well now, laughing and loving life again, and she's very excited about your wedding. She's something special, your Bubbie. I guess you're a lot like her because you're something special, too.

You and RC will have a book of all these pictures, so on rainy days you can sit by the fireplace and look and laugh and love and remember the joys of family and friends. In the meantime, remember that you and RC were friends before you decided to become a family. Cherish that friendship, the love and respect, the faith and belief, the patience and understanding. It will make your life rich forever and it will spill over and touch other lives and family and friends and you will be richer still.

In two short months I will walk you down the aisle. I will walk with my head held high. You are ready. You have learned important lessons. You have your toolbox for survival.

All I can say is, RC better be ready, too, or he'll have some explaining to do – to my brothers.

After all, what is family for?

MONEY

Many persons
have a wrong idea of what constitutes happiness.
It is not attained through self-gratification but through
fidelity to a worthy purpose.

HELEN KELLER

MONEY

Here's a riddle for you, kiddo. Is money good or bad?

The correct answer is: neither.

Money is only money. It's what you do with it that counts. But doesn't the Bible say that money is the root of all evil? No, actually the Bible says, "The love of money is the root of all evil." What that means is that God does not want you loving money more than Him or more than your husband or more than your family because when you love money more than anything else, you've got problems.

Look around. Every day is the nine-to-five rat race rush hour. What's that all about? Why are the rats racing and rushing so? Could it be the money? See, rats think money brings happiness and the more money they have the happier they'll be so they race around the maze of life trying to get more money so they'll be happier – but that doesn't work! They have more money and they have more things but they don't know their kids and they don't know each other and they don't have more happiness at all, they have emptiness.

Best as I can tell, happiness doesn't come from outside things. Happiness is an inside deal. It comes from balance and understanding and peace of mind. But if you're busy rat-racing around, looking for happiness in things and money, then you start making decisions based on things and money. That may be bottom line fine for business but living life is just a little bit different than doing business.

Then again, I'm just an old hippie. I used to think that money was bad because it looked like people were doing bad things with money. It took me until I was forty to realize it wasn't the money that was bad, it was the people. If bad people can do bad things with money, then good people should be able to do good things with money. I got a slow start but it never kept us from loving life and learning lessons and having lunch by a Connecticut waterfall or sunset on the Pacific. We didn't live our life based on money. We made our decisions based on doing the right thing and keeping our hearts in the right place and having fun, and that seemed to work out pretty good.

Now that I'm a little older and realize that money isn't evil, it's what you do with it, I think I'd like to have some more of it. There's a lot of living left, and money can help with education and travel and cars and homes, as well as building schools and libraries and supporting missionary work. And if you have your priorities straight, money can eliminate financial stress, and there seems to be a lot of rats suffering from that.

As far as money goes, it always seems like you need more no matter how much you have. But don't go rat-racing chasing money and miss the real stuff of life. Find a balance, do what you believe in your heart to be right and good, help others less fortunate along the way, give to the needy or your favorite charity. If you have your values right then money can't hurt you.

Today in America in the land of the free, people aren't free anymore because they're buried in debt. The banks own them. They have credit cards and bank loans and car leases and mortgages because Madison Avenue sold them a bill of goods, the "buy now pay later" lie. Don't fall into that trap, kiddo, then you become just another rat-racing, trying to stay ahead of the bill collectors. There is no peace of mind in debt. Papou always said cash was king and if you didn't have the money in your pocket then you didn't need it, whatever it was you wanted to buy.

The basics of money are like the basics of life, you've got to have a plan, in this case a budget. First off, make sure the first 10% goes to God because God made everything, including the money. He just wants to see your show of faith and then He will multiply what you have given and give it back to you. That's called, "tithing."

Then, save as much as you can, at least another 20% a week. Live below your means. You don't need flashy cars right now. When you have the cash in the bank and you've given to God and you want to buy a flashy car, then do it, pay cash. See, banks make all their money by loaning people money and collecting interest, and the last thing you want is to be paying interest all your life.

And the most important thing about money is, you want be in control of the money instead of the money being in control of you. If you're buried, in debt, then the money is controlling you. And nothing should control you in this life except for God and your commitment to your husband. Nothing.

So do the right thing by your God, your self and each other. I know that you and RC have done a ten year financial plan and I am so impressed and proud – and when you little CPA brainheads get it all figured out, maybe you can help your Dad.

In the meantime, remember the garden of life.

Sow good seeds and you will reap a good harvest.

RAGS make paper,

PAPER makes money,

MONEY makes banks,

BANKS make loans,

LOANS make beggars,

BEGGARS make RAGS.

--Anonymous, c. 18th century

CHOICE

Destiny is not a matter of chance, it is a matter of choice.
It is not a thing to be waited for;
it is a thing to be achieved.

WILLIAM JENNINGS BRYAN

CHOICE

To be or not to be, that is the question. Do they still teach Shakespeare in schools today? He has some profound insights into man and the human condition. He's right, life all comes down to choice. It's your life. What are you going to be – or not be? Your move.

See, when God made us He made hearts that pump and hands that hold and supercomputer brains to think and process and lungs to breathe and legs to carry and eyes to see and noses to smell and all this stuff we just take for granted. But He also gave us choice. We have the freedom to choose our own course in life, our own destination, our own goals, and our own dreams. He also gave us the freedom to choose what we believe. We can even *choose* to believe or not believe in God. So what do you want your life to be?

There are three kinds of people in this world; ones who make things happen and ones who watch things happen and ones who say, "what happened?". And you're the first kind. You make things happen. Most people choose not to choose and just sit there and let life happen and then they whine and complain and cry victim. Victim, my eyeball! They have the same freedom of choice as you, they just don't use it and that's their choice.

But that's not you. You have your Bubbie's and Papou's blood in you and they always believed in taking action and helping others in doing the right thing and that's how they raised me, and how I raised you. You were taught to be strong and good and honest and respectful and you are all that and a whole lot more. It was a miracle to see you born and it's still a miracle today watching you grow and develop into a strong, determined, thoughtful, considerate, loving, beautiful, graceful, diplomatic, caring, young woman.

It's amazing what you can grow in the garden of life with just a choice, a little effort and a lot of love. Let's say you're a seed, a tomato seed. I planted that seed twenty-four years ago and added water and light and fertilizer and did a little weeding. Then I stuck a pole in the ground for a little support and now there's this strong, vibrant, thriving tomato plant sending forth fruits day after day, year after year and inside each fruit is more seeds. There's this whole ripple effect of beauty and abundance that keeps coming every year from this one little seed. But if I didn't choose to plant the seed in the first place, twenty-four years ago, there would be no tomato today. Choices.

You've always got choices. You can't choose if it will rain or be sunny, so don't waste time being upset because you don't like the weather. But you can choose how you react so why not make the best of every situation. If life gives you lemons, make lemon meringue pie. And if life gives you limes, make a margarita.

Best as I can tell, we are what we choose to be and our lives are what we choose them to be, so if you look in the mirror and you don't like everything you see, don't panic, you can change. You have freedom of choice. And don't worry about making wrong choices. We all make wrong choices, that's how we learn. If you make a wrong choice, learn from it, make a correction, chart a new course and move on down the road. Remember "Tom Ed."

Do you remember when you were two and we were in New Haven, driving down the street and you were sitting in your little car seat right next to me? It was okay back then in '76 to have kids in the front seat. But this car swerved in front of us without using a turn signal. I don't like rude drivers so I opened my mouth and spit out some choice swear words. And you were just sitting there next to me, just learning to talk and you wanted to be just like your Dad so you said in your little kid voice, "swear word, swear word".

I had this revelation right there in the car on the streets of New Haven that everything I said you were going to say and everything I did you were going to do and I had a choice about what I was going to say and do. Did I want you to grow up swearing with a foul mouth or did I want to raise a young lady? So I made the choice to clean up my act and set the right example.

See, when you're a dad, you are responsible not only for your mouth but also for your kid's mouth and you are responsible not only for your own life but also for the life you brought into the world. That's a big responsibility. I had to think about everything I said and did because your life was depending on it. Choice.

Then back when you were five I had a major big choice. Your Mom had re-married and she and her new husband wanted to adopt you so I wouldn't be around. It was not a particularly friendly situation between the grown-ups as I'm sure you remember. Not all memories are happy. That's just life.

The choice was before me, to be or not to be. Was I going to be a good father or was I going to give up my rights and responsibilities? If I let you be adopted I would have no responsibilities, spiritual, financial or otherwise and I could return to L.A. and pursue my budding film career. But who in their right mind would choose to give up their child and pursue career goals instead of being a Dad?

I made my choice and moved to New York and hired lawyers to fight for my rights. Remember I said it wasn't a particularly friendly situation? The way it was in '79, the mother was always right and the father was always wrong but all I knew was I was your Dad and I would do my best regardless of the courts. It was a simple choice. I was your Dad and I couldn't desert you. If our kids are our future and our kids grow up feeling deserted and bad about themselves, then what does our future look like?

See, a Dad has to give his kid not only love and respect and guidance and faith and belief, but self-esteem too. How can you do anything in life if you don't believe in yourself? But you don't have to worry about self-esteem, kiddo. You've got it. I did my best to make sure of that. Remember the mountain? I gave you the choice to believe in yourself and you did. Right then and there you chose to believe in yourself. Life can never take that away from you.

I recall the mountains of Wyoming in my mind

when I walked you down the aisle and gave you away. I thank God every day for the fullness of our life and the joys and sorrows we've shared together. I am excited for you. You are a whole person, beautiful inside and out. You are ready, shaped by love and the fullness of life, to make your choices and live a good life of challenge and growth and struggle and joy. To the mountains.

Marriage will be a lifetime journey, take one step at a time. You will have choices to make every day, some little, some big. Each choice will be like a pebble in the water of life, the ripples will echo in your soul for a lifetime. Choose wisely.

Choose to find the good instead of finding the fault.

Choose to show praise and appreciation instead of criticism and disappointment.

Choose faith and belief instead of fear and doubt.

Choose to put each other up instead of putting each other down.

Choose respect and trust.

Choose love and understanding.

Choose to never take life for granted. Cherish each special moment and make the most of it.

Choose to laugh – a lot.

And finally, choose to call your Dad – at least once a week.

I love you kiddo. *You da best!*

DREAMS

Quitters never win
and winners never quit.

VINCE LOMBARDI

DREAMS

When we're kids and we're little, we all have dreams of how we want to grow up and how we want our lives to be. And then we grow up and become adults. We hit a few stumbling blocks and skin a few knees and have to cope with loss and failure, and a lot of people just flat out give up on their dreams and settle for whatever life will give them. It takes hard work and perseverance to make those dreams we dreamed come true, and most people would rather channel surf than follow their dream.

But God made a miracle when He made you and I sure didn't raise you to be a quitter. Only a few people go to the top of the mountain because most people aren't willing to pay the price. But you are one of the few. You've already been to the top and you know what it takes to get there. You have paid the price. You know what it looks like from the top. You are a winner.

When you were born I didn't know really what it meant to be a father but I was still excited and had a dream for you. I didn't dream that you would be a great scientist and discover the cure for cancer or invent and design a pollution-free solar car. My dream was simple. I just dreamed that you would grow up to be a good person and help make the world a little bit better just by being here.

And you know what? My dream came true. You, my kid, my precious little wonderment of God looking through that crescent moon in your mahogany cradle, you are a dream come true woman.

You're loving. I see how you are with me and RC and Bubbie and your uncles and aunts and sisters and brother and friends. I see how caring and thoughtful and considerate and respectful and loving you are. Don't think I don't see. I'm your Dad, remember?

You're strong. When you make your mind up, kiddo, it's a done deal. I see that. When you graduated UGA you had your mind set on getting a new car and driving cross-country. You did exactly that. You bought your car all on your own and packed your little sister in there with you and drove cross-country from Atlanta to the Pacific staying with friends and family and visiting the great National Parks and Monuments and back to

Atlanta again. You're incredible. Don't think I don't see that.

You have style. You and RC have already bought and decorated your first home and your choice of fabrics and furniture and Southwest artifacts are terrific. Where did you learn all that? When I was married, I had a ponytail and wore bell bottom pants and beads, your Mom and I had an electric spool for a kitchen table and cinder blocks and boards for bookshelves. And we thought that was "cool".

Of course, I could go on and on but then you'd get a big head. I just want you to know that you are a dream come true and when I walk you down the aisle this June I know in my heart of hearts without the shadow of a doubt that I will be giving away one wonderful woman. You will be a wonderful wife, a caring friend, a thoughtful companion, a strong and dynamic partner for life. Does RC know how lucky he is marrying you? He'd better, or I'll have my brothers talk to him.

Anyway, my dream of being a good Dad and raising up a good person has come true and I've got some other dreams I've got to take care of now. But the main thing for you and RC is your dreams, kiddo.

Know that you are ready. You've got the toolbox for survival, it's in your heart and in your soul and you can do anything that you put your mind to. I believe in you one hundred percent, but it's just like back on the mountain, it's not what I believe, it's what you believe and if you believe you can do it, then you can do it. No doubt about it.

Remember the stories we made up when you were little about Rutabaga Marmalada and her dad, Oingo Boingo and the First World Children's Circus and the little poem she had about life. It went like this . . .

> Travel the path with heart
> living life is but an art.
> It's all up to you
> to put on your shoe,
> so travel the path with heart.

Well, put on your shoe, kiddo, here comes the road of life. Just hold hands and be friends.

> Believe in each other
> and
> respect each other
> and
> forgive each other

and

pray a lot

and

play a lot

and

laugh a lot

and

love a lot

and

you kids will do just fine.

I believe in you, kiddo, always have and always will. So put on your shoes and go out there and get 'em. You can do it.

And don't forget, call your Dad.
Because I said so.

Love and hugs,
you da best,

ORDER FORM

THE WORLD ACCORDING TO DAD FOR NEWLYWEDS

To order more copies of *DAD,* call 1-800-431-1579 or visit our web site at www.worlddad.com

Quantity ($12.00 each)	
Shipping & Handling	
Subtotal	
Sales Tax (Virginia 4.5%)	
Total Enclosed	

Please enclose $4.20 to cover shipping and handling for the first book and $1.00 for each additional copy, only applying to the same address.

Name:
Address:
City, State, Zip
Telephone No:

and for your friends:

Name:
Address:
City, State, Zip
Telephone No:

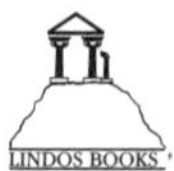

To write or email the author use the addresses below.

LINDOS BOOKS • 17956 Canby Road, Leesburg, VA. 20175
Tel: • 540.338.1152 • Email • dad@worlddad.com • Fax • 540.338.5966